*To my family,
past, present, and future.*

Copyright © 2014 by Rosetree, LLC

All rights reserved.

ISBN 978-1-312-03156-2

First Edition

Grow Up & Herd Cats
A Handbook for First-Time Managers

by Joshua M. Rosenbaum

"Management is nothing more than motivating other people."

- Lee Iacocca

Table of Contents

Author's Note .... p. 5

Introduction .... p. 8

Chapter 1: The Rules .... p. 12

Chapter 2: A Little More Tough Love .... p. 20

Chapter 3: Things to Ponder .... p. 23

Before You Go... .... p. 43

Author's Note

As an author, I'm sticking to one of the lessons I've learned about being a manager - namely, just because the ideas in this book are mine doesn't mean they are right. Feel free to take what you read with a grain of salt, or completely disagree with whatever you will. I encourage it. I'm just sharing what I think I know, and trying to get people talking and communicating and thinking and growing. That's what becoming a good manager demands of all of us who try (and I am by no means finished learning about becoming a good manager!). I'm open to everyone's opinion, and may even be convinced to change my own about a thing or two.

Should you have contradictory feelings about anything I say in this book I encourage you to debate the point out in the open. Talk about it with the people around you who care to listen. Discuss it with me and others on my blog www.growupandherdcats.com so we can all hear your thoughts and get in on the debate.

"Advice in old age is foolish; for what can be more absurd than to increase our provisions for the road the nearer we approach to our journey's end."

-Marcus Tullius Cicero

Introduction

In today's internet enabled, idea-centric economy, you don't have to be old and experienced to be boss. For decades, managers were made from the people who climbed the corporate ladder, slogging for years up the pay grade as they waited for someone to die, quit, get fired or relocated resulting in a management position to be filled. Everybody gunned for the management jobs. Positions went to those who had the experience, those who were "in with the boss," those who put in the time at the company, or the people whose tenure provided them with seniority. In other words, management was typically for older folks.

Today you can develop a product, start a business, and be the CEO of a company with 200 staff all before you finish college (or drop out). This has become commonplace all over the world. But what's happening even more frequently is that young, exuberant 20-somethings are being hired for salaried jobs, often their first "real" job, and rapidly they are getting bumped up into a management position. Often it's only after performing at their job for several months or a year. Businesses are growing and adding staff so rapidly in the tech industry that a career track that used to take five years is commonly happening in two. It's the norm to see a startup go from 5 people to 65 in a year or two. Growth is prevalent, rapid, and it's not going to stop in the near future.

Which brings us back to why I've written this book, what it is, and who it's for. This is a handbook for first time managers. Managers who haven't spent the past five or ten years working the same job at the same company under the same boss or two. Managers who haven't yet put in the years it takes to experience what it means to be a good boss or a bad one. Managers who still are trying to figure out what they are really good at, what they suck at, what they can fake and what they don't understand. Managers who don't quite know themselves yet, who haven't worked above, below, or alongside enough various characters in different professional situations to know how to navigate the individual personalities and challenges that human emotion imposes on the workplace.

As I mentioned earlier, this is not a how-to book. It's not the next great revelation about tactics, performance, or metaphorical and metaphysical strategies for leadership. It is merely a set of mantras, statements, observations, and tough love that should act as a guide along your journey towards becoming a great manager.

That journey needs to be short, because people's livelihoods are at stake, and those livelihoods are very much in your hands!

Keep this little handbook on your desk, in your purse or in your pocket. Peruse it when you have a few spare minutes, or when you need a break. Refer to it during challenging moments. Hand it to someone at work who may be stressed out or anxious about how they're doing. Quote from it when helping someone through a crisis. Give it as a gift to your friend who was just promoted to Manager, For The First Time.

Good luck becoming a great manager.

"Without continual growth and progress, such words as improvement, achievement, and success have no meaning."

- Benjamin Franklin

Chapter 1:
The Rules

Let's get one thing out of the way. This is a tough love kind of book, so I'm not pulling any punches. If you want the soft sell, go read something else. There are plenty of books on management, and most of them wind up saying the same thing, the only difference being what metaphors the author uses to make you believe his way is different, or new, or in some cases, revolutionary. I'm not knocking those books, or their authors, I'm sure some of them are good and you could benefit from reading them. But I just ask that you read this one first, because it won't take long and it gets right to the point.

This is a handbook and as such it's short. The reason it's short is that I've cut through the crap and have provided you with the just the basic ideals that are necessary to become a good manager. You have no time to waste, and I don't want you to get bogged down in theories and steps and complicated dogma. I also don't want you jumping the gun and getting swept up in the positive results and Limitless Potential of Being a Great Corporate Leader! before you see the battlefield for what it really is.

It's way too easy to get tapped for a management job and start out with all the right intentions and gather up all the "correct" information and get started only to find yourself three weeks in pissing people off and becoming a dick without even realizing it.

That's the slippery slope. When you get that title bestowed unto you there is a dose of power that comes with it. And power, however small, is power; and as such it has the unlimited potential to fuck up everybody's if not wielded wisely.

There are three rules I'm going to ask that you follow as a reader of this handbook. I ask this of you not because I like following rules (in fact just the opposite), but because if you don't follow these three rules, this handbook won't do you any good. You'll probably feel offended, depressed, possibly talked down to, and maybe antagonized unless you absorb and follow these rules while reading. It's a lot to ask, I know, but there's one other reason I need you to follow these rules, and it is this:

These three rules that you'll need to follow while reading the book are critical, and will apply just as well, to your job as manager. So it's like a two for one deal you're getting here. That's the bargain. May as well start practicing while you read this little book. Besides, if this little book tests your patience, then you can chuck it across the room and pick it up when you've collected yourself. Might be good practice for things to come. And those things *will* come.

So enough of that, let's get to it. Here are the rules:

Rule I: Adopt Humility

The First Rule you must follow as a reader of this book and as a manager is to adopt humility. Breathe in a healthy lungful of it. Now hold your breath and let it all get absorbed into your bloodstream. You're going to need lots and lots of this stuff, trust me.

Sure, you can congratulate yourself on your promotion and feel good about yourself for a day or two, or a weekend. But when it comes time to get to work in your new position as manager, the suit you need to put on under those fancy new clothes, and wear every single day, are the Long Johns of Humility.

Humility shall be the foundation you stand upon for the rest of your career as manager. It will help you to listen, to process, and to behave, which make up most of the motions you go through between the big management decisions. These are the things you do that comprise the bulk of your job on a day to day basis, and, they mostly mean *engaging with other people*. Adopting humility now, full-heartedly, will ensure you don't make the common mistake of thinking that because some of these people are now below you on the org chart, they are below you as human beings. This happens all too easily and all too often. So put on those long johns, and get comfortable wearing them. After a while, you shouldn't even realize you have them on.

Rule II: Suck It Up

Your Second Rule as reader/manager is this: If you are going to be sensitive or put off by being told you are wrong, that you're a failure, or worse, nothing at all because they aren't talking *to* you they are talking *about* you and you don't know if what *they* are saying is *good* or *bad*, then you need to immediately begin practicing an important exercise I call *Suck It Up*.

This exercise is critical because during your future career as a manager, there's going to be lots of it to do. So start practicing now.

The tone of my prose may help - if it is putting you off, *suck it up*. Pretty please, with sugar on top.

Which brings us to the Third Rule. An old professor of mine once said to me,

> *"I may not always be right, and you can always disagree with what I'm telling you. But first you must shut up and accept what I'm telling you, and do as I say. After you've finished doing that, you can question everything and disagree all you want."*

This statement directly confronts the idea of social hierarchy. If we were apes living in a jungle, this next rule wouldn't apply. But we aren't apes in a jungle, we are people, who despite our standing in society or in the workplace will only succeed if we conquer our inner primates and do the one thing only humans can, and must do...

Rule III: Grow Up

There's one thing you must do above all else in order to prepare yourself for what you are about to take on, and it is this: *Grow Up.*

Becoming a manager means you are now a parent. Your staff are your children. Their livelihoods are in your hands. Their happiness and productivity and plans and dreams and goals are now all your responsibility.

That isn't to say you must *make* them happy, productive, and make their plans and dreams and goals come true. It *is* to say that you are responsible for providing them with the correct environment in which they can achieve those things. *You* hired them (or your company did, no matter), and *you* are their manager, so your job is *to enable them to be the best version of the person you hired, and do what you hired them to do*.

Growing up usually involves making sacrifices

for the benefit of others. Sometimes having the upper hands means knowing when to let the other guy win. And that doesn't always mean that by doing so, you lose. You are now more than ever part of a team, and your job is to make that team a highly productive group of highly productive individuals. So you will quickly need to learn that the people on your team come first, and that might take sacrifice. But as you mature as a manager, those sacrifices will be fewer and less painful. In fact they may not even hurt at all.

It helps to know that management is the long game, so play it that way. Keep your eyes on the horizon line, and help the soldiers at your side get you there.

Chapter 2:
A Little More Tough Love

It may sound exciting and wonderful to have been chosen to become a manager. The prestige, the acknowledgment, the salary bump, etc. But all that comes at a cost that you may or may not realize yet, and it is this: If at some point down the line anyone you are responsible for becomes unhappy, frustrated, or unproductive, guess what: It's *your* fault. Not their fault, and not the company's fault. It is *your* fault.

So here come the reflexive *Buts*. You might say, *"But they just don't seem to be happy doing what I hired them to do!"*

Well then find out why, and fix it. Check your emotions and biases and ego at the door and start politely investigating. Tune in and listen. Ask the right people the right questions and you will figure it out, I assure you - and rather quickly I might add.

You may also say, *"But the company has changed so much, it's not my fault they don't like how it is around here nowadays."*

Horsehockey. If the company changes, then you must mitigate that change on behalf of your staff. Own it. It doesn't mean you work alone or have to fix everything yourself. It means you actively seek out the pain points with everyone you manage. You work with the group as a whole, and you guide everyone as selflessly as possible into a happy, productive place, throughout the change.

If there is one operational message that you glean from this handbook, it is this: *If something is off, find out why, and fix it.*

Like parenting, it takes a lot of acceptance to be selfless and content, but when you realize the richness of the rewards, i.e. the gratitude, happiness, and loyalty of another human being, and a well performing team, it becomes a heck of a lot easier.

"We cannot seek achievement for ourselves and forget about progress and prosperity for our community... Our ambitions must be broad enough to include the aspirations and needs of others, for their sakes and for our own."

- Cesar Chavez

Chapter 3:
Things to Ponder

The following pages are merely ideas and thoughts, observations and tips that might help fortify the foundations you will need to build to support your future efforts. Hopefully they are easy to grasp but full of meaning.

Blaze through them once, or take it a page or a section at a time, and let them marinate for a while before moving on. Whichever way you decide to approach this chapter is up to you, but it's really the stuff that I hope you take with you for the rest of your career. Maybe 20 years from now when you are a CEO you'll stumble across this little handbook and chuckle. You can thank me later.

Management

Managing means putting the company first, your staff second, and yourself third.

Be selfish to your boss. Be selfless with your staff.

A boss answers to no one. A manager answers to everyone.

You're not right, just because you're the manager.

People's jobs are their livelihoods. You cannot take that seriously enough.

Your first job is to listen to your boss, and report to her that everything is on track and going well. Your second job is to communicate what your boss told you to each of your staff in a way that they understand. Your third job is to provide each of them what they need in order to perform at their best.

Managers are not allowed to whine to anybody except other managers. And even that's a bad idea.

"Flat" organizations only work at small scale. Above 50 people they fail for the same reasons communism did.

Think hard about why you were given the job of manager. Was it because you had seniority? Was it because you were good at performing your last job? Was it because you have an MBA? Was it because you had previous experience at managing people? Now go ask your boss point blank why he gave you that position. Then compare your answer with his.

If you were made manager because you performed well at your job, you are most likely in trouble.

If you were made manager because you had seniority, you may be in a little trouble.

If you were made manager because you had previous experience managing people, you may be ok.

If you were made manager just because you have an MBA, you could be screwed.

Skills

Some people are natural managers. These are rare people.

If you've never had a good manager, you don't know what a good manager is.

If you've never had a bad manager, you don't know what a good manager is.

Your age *can* have something to do with it. It can work for you, it can work against you. Wield it wisely.

If you've never owned a business and worked for yourself, there are some things you absolutely do not know. Listen out for them.

People

The goal of any smart organization is to maintain a happy, productive workforce. Whatever boss said that they don't care about the happiness of their staff is a fool.

Happy, productive workers perform better and last longer than unhappy, productive workers. Unhappy workers spread unhappiness and then they leave, or get fired, and turnover is expensive.

High turnover is bad for business.

Loyalty is a bedrock of happiness and performance.

People at work are not loyal to a brand, a mascot, a benefits package, or a salary. They are loyal to other people.

Be loyal to each individual on your staff, and they will be loyal to you. Find ways to show your loyalty. A great way to do that is by asking them questions often, and listening to their answers.

Everyone is different, but people *do* fall into a handful of categories when it comes to their workplace personality characteristics. There are several systems, i.e. Myers-Briggs, that use testing to categorize and label the workplace personality characteristics of different people.

As controversial as these methods are, they work. They may not be 100% accurate, but they certainly help. They particularly help managers understand how to communicate with different individuals depending on their workplace personality type.

Managing people is an entirely different animal than managing a process, a facility, a business, or having technical skills. Managing people is like herding cats.

Cats can choose to follow you, or you can lure them into following you. End of story.

For simplicity's sake, let's accept the fact that you cannot change people (internal factors).

Behavior, on the other hand, can be modified.

Behavior is how people react to their environments (external factors). Therefore, in order to modify people's behavior, change their environments.

There are incentives that work for everyone. It is your job to know what they are and how and when to apply them.

Sometimes the difference between a happy worker and an unhappy one is a job title.

Money goes a long way towards soothing a frustrated worker. However it is only a temporary solution.

Benefits are sometimes worth more than a salary.

You may make the final decisions, but those decisions belong to your team, so you better hope they are happy with them.

Any time you leave somebody out, they are going to think its ok to leave you out.

Communication

Your most important tool is your ability to clearly and effectively communicate with each and everyone individual you manage.

Communication is your best friend. Especially when it seems like the hardest thing to do.

It is your responsibility to communicate with someone who isn't communicating with you.

99% of all problems are caused by poor communication. 100% of those problems are your fault.

As a manager you should be talking 20% of the time. The other 80% should be spent listening. Of that 80%, 20% of it should be spent listening to your boss, and 80% to your staff.

You need to communicate regularly with everyone. Even if it feels unnecessary.

If you don't know something, you need to ask at least two people for the answer.

If you have to mitigate a problem between people on your team, you need to do it with both of them in the room at the same time.

Be as transparent as possible, all the time.

Treat everyone who works under you as if they are your boss, or your client.

Respect everybody, all of the time.

Managers always have work to do. If you don't, go talk to your staff and see if there's anything you can do to help.

If someone on your team doesn't have enough work to do, talk to them, you'll come up with something.

Nobody's opinion is wrong.

Problems

If you've given the same apology more than once, you are the problem.

If someone you manage has a problem, it is your problem, and, if you do not fix it, your fault.

If any part of a staff member's life-work balance is off, it is your responsibility to do whatever you can to help fix it. Let *them* tell you it's none of your business.

Managers can never, ever blame someone on their team for a failure. Failures are the managers fault. However, successes are to be shared by everyone.

Unless someone is lazy, destructive, or a liar, their lack of performance is your fault.

Unless they are lazy, destructive, or lied on their resume, if you have to let someone go, you've failed.

If someone is frustrated with their job, it is your duty to do whatever is in your power to alleviate the conditions that frustrate them.

Managers know when to support cliques and

when to bust them up. However if cliques are ever a problem, it is your fault. And cliques are always a problem, because by definition there are people who are not in them, and no one likes not being in the clique (even if they say they do).

Your toughest challenge will be dealing with this case:

There is one person on your team who performs well, but no one gets along with. If this happens, try and expose a common interest outside of work (by sanctioning some out of office social activities or events) and hope for the best.

If you think someone just isn't working out, try again. If it still isn't working out, try again.

If someone isn't busy enough for long enough they will begin to feel insecure about their job. Talk to them often until the problem is solved.

Check your emotions at the door when you get to work. Except the happy ones.

You are not allowed to get upset with anyone you manage.

Every problem is yours to solve. So don't cause more of them.

Life is too short, and it's just a job. Have fun.

Before You Go...

After all these quips, observations, and bits of tough love, you may be feeling a little despondent, or nervous about what's to come. If you really took those three rules to heart, maybe less so. Either way, I'm here to tell you that being a manager does come with its rewards.

I'm not simply referring to the potential bump in pay, or the prestige on your resume; I'm talking about the sense of fulfillment you may experience when you have a team of happy, highly performing people that all see you as a positive, supportive pillar around which they spend their day doing their business for the common good. Earning the respect of your peers is exponentially better than expecting it because of a job title, and getting there may take some time but the path travelled will always be its own reward. It isn't as daunting as I may have made it sound, and although it will certainly take a sustained effort, you *can* do it, and it *will* be worth it.

Make *becoming a great manager* your goal every day. It takes no money, no permission, no board decisions, and no degree to achieve. If you do, the rewards will keep coming.

Now go out there and get 'em.

"Instead of being critical of people in authority over you and envious of their position, be happy you're not responsible for everything they have to do. Instead of piling on complaints, thank them for what they do. Overwhelm them with encouragement and appreciation!"

- Joyce Meyer

Happy managing!

About the Author

Joshua M. Rosenbaum is a creative professional, web cinematographer and a father currently living in Atlanta, Georgia with his fiancé Sharon. He can also be found spending time with his son who lives in Moorsel, Belgium.

visit www.growupandherdcats.com

For further info and queries please email
josh@growupandherdcats.com

©2014, Rosetree, LLC. All Rights Reserved.

www.ingramcontent.com/pod-product-compliance
Lightning Source LLC
Chambersburg PA
CBHW070432180526
45158CB00017B/1096